THE KEY TO HAPPINESS

They will never affect you emotionally again

Harry Specter

Harry Specter ...

My only goal is that each of my books help you to become the best version of yourself, I only give you the knowledge but do not forget that all change will depend on you. And when this happens I want you to feel proud of yourself, and if you could achieve all that, imagine what you can do in a few years ...

This is one of the many books that I have, I recommend you buy all of them for a better understanding, don't worry, they are at a very low price, but their value is too high.

What I teach is not a mystical exercise, but a set of practical tools to teach you to act effectively overcoming any fear that we harbor.

When you have finished reading this book, you will know how to get yourself into a state of peak performance and capacity whenever you want, and how to get out of disabling states. Remember that the key to power is action. My goal is to share with you how the statements that lead to decisive, consistent and responsible action are used.

The key to happiness

"Do not expect everything to change, while you remain the same person"

What a vision means ... everyone has wishes.

Desire is an incremental way to improve our life.

Today you wish, I must have a home, tomorrow you wish, I must have this money, tomorrow, you want something more. These are incremental ways of organizing and rearranging our lives, which are needed to get a few things done.

When they say that I am a visionary, what they are saying is, I have a greater desire that is not just about the incremental improvement of my life.

Desire is on me, always.

Vision is a process of total inclusion. So this in itself is a phenomenal thing, if people instead of having desires, if they have a vision; the vision is always fully inclusive.

The desire is personal. Desire leads to incremental changes and improvements.

Vision can transform the whole situation.

So, about the will. To be a volunteer, a volunteer means someone who is doing something voluntarily, right? There is no other compulsion. There are no financial compulsions, there are no social compulsions, there is nothing else.

You want to do something of your own free will.

So when you are a self-willed person. I ask you this question, right now, are you obliged to read my book or are you reading it of your own free will? Voluntarily.

Because I have also talked to people who do their military service. I have spoken in prisons, I have spoken in many places.

So you are here of your own free will.

You are doing something voluntarily, it is the foundation of your joy, isn't it?

As simple or stupid or idiotic as the activity

is, "I'm doing something voluntarily" makes a

world of difference, doesn't it?

Yes

The difference between heaven and hell is just

this. You are doing something voluntarily,

that is your heaven.

You are doing something involuntarily, that is

your hell.

We have already taken attitudes: what we like and what we don't like. I like this person, I don't like this person.

Now with this person, I will do things voluntarily. With this person, I will do things involuntarily.

This can be two people, two aspects of life, two communities, two nations, two ... many things.

This I will do voluntarily, this I will do involuntarily. This means, "I have decided in my mind, this is good, this is bad."

When I hear, even on the national news channels, good people and bad people ... it's just ... once you have this kind of issue, you will be disastrous for the planet. It's just a matter of time.

The moment you decide that this is a good person, this is a bad person ... this has deeply penetrated world society.

Do not.

There are no good people and no bad people.

Everyone is oscillating between the two. If you create a very nice and wonderful environment, everyone will behave wonderfully.

If you create an unpleasant atmosphere,

many people act nasty.

Yes or no?

There are happy people and miserable people,

but there are no good and bad people.

The moment we think we are good, we have

the right to destroy the bad, right?

Oh, we've been destroying a lot of people for a long time, it's time to stop that.

Because...

Human beings are at different levels of experience and understanding.

Variety of people. Anyone who's not like you is obviously bad, isn't he? It is not like this?

Those who are not like me must be bad

people.

Because the basis of goodness and what you

think goodness is is decided by you.

No, it's none of your business to do that.

Will means this.

I'm just willing.

I am one hundred percent yes to life.

I am not "yes to this, no to this."

No, I'm just yes and yes to life.

If you are one hundred percent yes to life, you are a volunteer.

You have become a willing life.

You have become so willing that you have no will of your own.

People ask me "Specter, how do you deal with all these people, all kinds of horrible questions that they are asking, are they doing this, are they doing that? "

I said 'My life is not about them. It's about me

»

It's about how I am. This is about me. No matter what they are, that is your choice.

But how I am is my choice. This is my way. It doesn't matter what they do. I am so.

Because I have not given that freedom to anyone that someone can upset me, someone can make me angry, someone can make me happy,

someone can make me unhappy.

These privileges I kept to myself.

It is time for you to do the same.

Because if someone else can decide what can happen inside of you right now, isn't this the ultimate bondage? Hmm? It is not?

Someone else can decide what should happen inside of you, what happens around you, of course, many people decide,

What happens around us is not one hundred percent ours, but what happens inside me must be my creation, right?

Right now, almost anyone can upset someone because they are not volunteers.

They are not ready.

So people keep coming up to me every day, "Specter, I can't work with this person, she's so horrible, I can't do it."

I tell them: "Look, in this world, these are the kind of people that exist; Well, well, well, well, these are the kind of people out there.

But if you want to work with ideal people, you must go to heaven and today.

But if you think that what you are doing is very significant, you must learn to work with all these horrible people.

This is how the world is.

If you think that what you are doing is very significant, you learn to work with all kinds of people.

You see, horrible people will do wonderful things.

Yes?

But if you want to work with ideal people, you won't find any.

I haven't found one yet.

There are all kinds of ... "mixed bags." but if you are willing, that you are not yes and no, yes to one, not to another, you are simply a great Yes, you will find a way.

Final message...

Take action. Undertake. Take responsibility.
Use what you have learned here, and do it
right away. And not only for yourself: also for
others.

The benefit of such actions is greater than
what you can imagine. In the world there are
many people who speak. Many know what is
right and what empowers, and yet they don't
get the results they want.

It is not enough to talk to walk the path; you have to start walking.

If this book helps you move in the right direction, I will indeed consider myself very lucky.

In the meantime, I thank you for your interest in learning, progressing and developing, and also for allowing me to share with you some of the principles that have made such a difference in my life.

May your search for human excellence be fruitful and permanent. May you dedicate yourself not only to fighting for the objectives that you have proposed, but also to considering others once the first ones have been achieved; not only to be faithful to his dreams of the past, but to dream of bigger ones still, and not only to take from this life what he can, but to love and live with generosity.

See you soon, and God bless you ...

The Key to Happiness by Harry Specter